Bloom

James McInerney

COVER DESIGN : ETHAN McINERNEY

Also by James McInerney

In Between the Lines

Dedicated to, as always,
Terri, Ethan and Erin.

BLOOM

BLACK BUTTERFLY

A SEA FULL OF ENDLESS WAVES

PULL ME DOWN

THE FAMILIAR ACHE

BROKEN PIECES

DAY ZERO

FRAGMENTED

ENDLESS GREY

THE CHASE

LETTING GO

FLOWERS

THE JOURNEY

THE FIRES THAT BURN

ADRIFT

SHE

LET IT BE

THE SEA

SO VERY DEEPLY

A GIRL

BLANK SPACES

APPRECIATE THE JOURNEY

MY SKY … MY STAR

I SIT AND WAIT

I CIRCLE IN YOUR ORBIT

ONE LAST TIME

LIVE FOR THE MOMENT

YOU ARE THE SKY

ANGEL

WILD

FOREVER GREEN

KNOWING I COULD WATCH YOU LEAVE

A REASON TO CHANGE

THIS IS HOW I MOVE

YOU ARE THE OCEAN

ROAD MAP

SMILE

RECKLESS HEART

NEXT TO YOU

GATHERED

THE FEAR

HIDDEN AWAY

PIECES

GRACE

DIAMONDS

UNTIL THE END

BURNT

FOUND MYSELF, FOUND YOU

WIDE AWAKE

BROKEN RECORD

THESE ARE NOT MY WORDS

FIRES

I SHALL WALK THIS PATH

SUCH PRECIOUS THINGS

STONES

BLOOM

PETRICHOR

THE FALL

A DARKENED CLOUD

STARS

SLOW DANCE

BATTLE SCARS

MY ANGEL

IF THE WORLD SHOULD CEASE TO BE

GENTLE

INFINITY

SOFTLY INTO THE NIGHT

THE THINGS WE LEAVE BEHIND

I AM KING

THE CROW

I FOUND MYSELF TODAY

MORNING SUN

I DARE NOT DREAM

JAGGED EDGES

GOD

ALL AT ONCE

TODAY WAS BUT A DREAM

PIECES OF ME

NIGHT AND DAY

MASQUERADE

STRANGERS

BROKEN

AN OLD FLAME

I AM BUT A LEAF

WITHIN MY HANDS

BEAUTIFUL

NEVER BE AFRAID

I STILL AWAKE EACH NIGHT

SILOHUETTE

LET IT RAIN

WINGS

I HAVE DREAMT

ROOTS

FOOTPRINTS IN THE SAND

THE DANCE

THE STRUGGLE

"Only take the words from this book that you need to repair the parts of yourself that love broke. When we carry things with us on our journey that have no use other than to weigh us down, they always sit heavy upon the heart."

— James McInerney

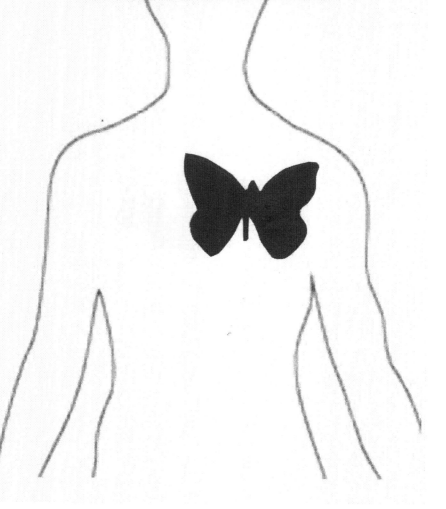

BLACK BUTTERFLY

'Black Butterfly'

I felt it all with you. The sorrow that never seemed to leave regardless of all the places I hid myself, knowing I would never belong. And yet I still hid. I endured the isolation. The memories that tore me apart, only to find that I was just as lost as when I was with you. Hammering on the invisible walls, my fists pounding the surface in the hope someone would save me from myself, that someone would notice that I still belonged, but no one ever did. So I stopped. I allowed the silence to cling to me in the way that I once held onto you, foolishly thinking it would last forever, only to realise my mistake.

#blackbutterfly

A SEA
FULL OF
ENDLESS
WAVES

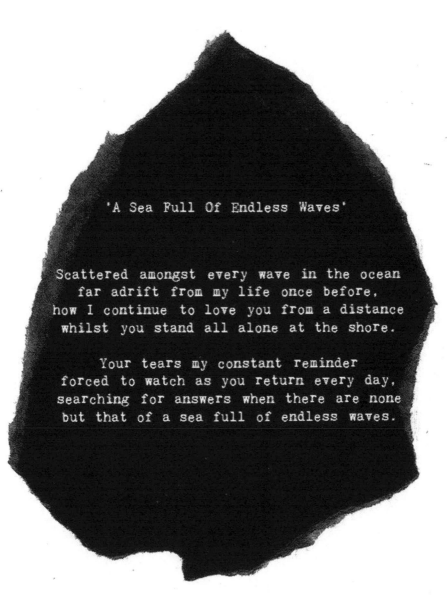

'A Sea Full Of Endless Waves'

Scattered amongst every wave in the ocean
far adrift from my life once before,
how I continue to love you from a distance
whilst you stand all alone at the shore.

Your tears my constant reminder
forced to watch as you return every day,
searching for answers when there are none
but that of a sea full of endless waves.

#aseafullofendlesswaves

'Pull Me Down'

Pull me down to where
you lay, for life has
no meaning if you
cannot stay. I will
close my eyes and fall
asleep, may beautiful
flowers forever grow
at my feet.

#pullmedown

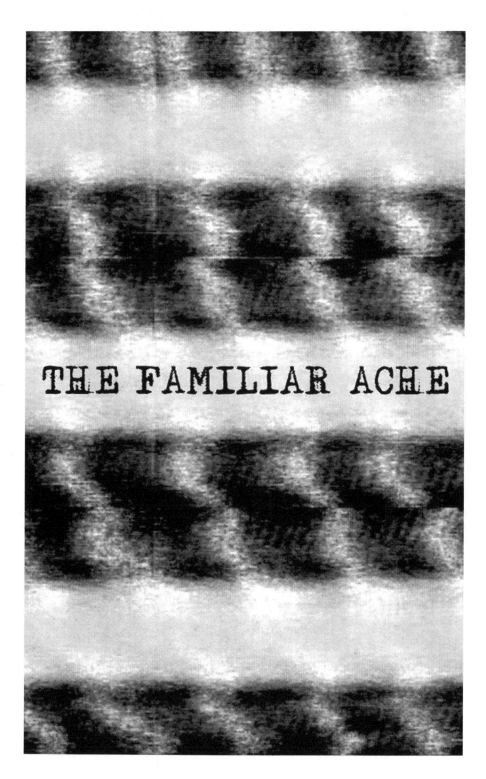

THE FAMILIAR ACHE

'The Familiar Ache'

And yet there is still an ache. An orchestra missing an instrument, a sunny day lacking warmth. What of those subtle differences? I dare say that to the watching audience, the music sounds perfect, yet to the conductor it's an incomplete piece that will never be noticed by anyone but him. You will awake and smile because the world expects it so, but like the lack of warmth on a sunny day, a smile without love behind it is just that: hollow, empty and vacant. The way your temporary period of loneliness will feel as your heart beats twice as fast to make up for the loss.

#theache

BROKEN
PIECES

'Broken Pieces'

I have lived albeit short yet
I feel as old as time, for an
eternity I've walked counting
every single mile. Although
my body never tires I fear my
heart is fading fast,
scattered fragments of me now
remain like a trail upon my
path. And I sometimes often
wonder, regardless of where I
roam, do you still collect
all my broken pieces and
continue to add them to your
own?

#brokenpieces

'Day Zero'

I'm letting you go
one breath at a time
recalling all our memories in reverse
as they erase from my mind,
then I won't have to miss you
I'll feel nothing at all
we'll just become strangers
who no longer collide
regardless of the fall.

#dayzero

FRAG
MENT
ED

'Fragmented'

I'm reminded of you as
though you were a cycle
of continuous thoughts,
each one seamlessly
connected to the other
like they belonged. And
yet we couldn't be more
fragmented, the bitter
pill already swallowed,
its taste lingering
longer than you ever
did.

#fragmented

ENDLESS GREY

'Endless Grey'

If there should ever
come a day that you and
I no longer share the
same sky, I will close
my eyes forever before
the beauty starts to
fade. Like a painted
picture formed, awash
with hope in darkened
shades, I won't marvel
at the world for it
shall be nothing but a
mass of endless greys
without you.

#endlessgrey

THE CHASE

'The Chase'

You will always be the calming waves
that keep me afloat as I endure the
chaos. There are no tides strong
enough nor does a sea exist as vast or
as endless like that of my love for
you. Yet I surrender all that I am as
though powerless, allowing the current
to hold me in the way you once did -
ferocious and wild. Without struggle
or sound I submit complete, knowing it
will be you who saves me, parting land
and sky with such passion to remind
the world I am yours. But I won't be
easily saved, I'll be defiant without
reason, a worthy pursuit for your love
in the hope you will never grow tired
of the chase.

#thechase

LETTING GO

'Letting Go'

Letting go is
impossible when
there are no
goodbyes.

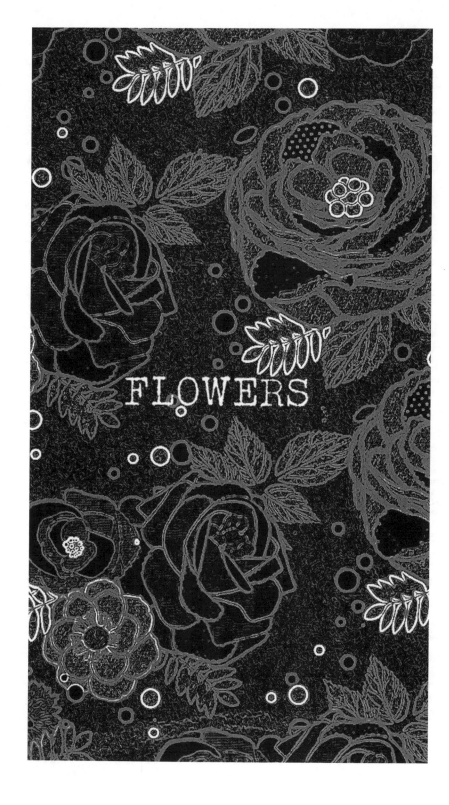

'Flowers'

Don't give yourself
up so easily when
love is involved.
There will always
be admirers of
beautiful flowers,
yet they won't
appreciate the
struggle that comes
before the bloom.

#flowers

THE
JOURNEY

'The Journey'

You are the Journey. A path I'm destined to travel when the timing is right. And it will be right, just not right now because right now we are two different people living different lives … worlds apart. And I know you get that feeling like you are the missing piece of a bigger picture, the constant hunger that never truly feels fulfilled. Worry not my dear, fight it every day with all that you are and never give up; I promise the best is yet to come. And though you will love others, probably with all of your heart because you are a good person, it won't be the kind of love that we will share. It will be different. Eternal. So live, laugh, love and enjoy your life and we will meet someday, somewhere in the middle and know instantly without words being said that it was worth the wait. That it was meant to be. That we were both on a journey. The greatest journey of our lives.

#thejourney

THE
FIRES
THAT
BURN

'The Fires That Burn'

I am nothing without your love, but a series of empty spaces that collide in the way we once did. Each lingering pause, a reminder of the emptiness that remains even though the fires in my heart still burn for you.

#firesburn

'Adrift'

I still remain in all the
places you once belonged,
upon an ocean filled with
memories that weigh me
down. You were always an
island of promise I would
drift towards, without
compass or winds to guide
my sail. And yet I now
move against the tide, a
raging storm in which I'm
held, the sea once a
paradise born to explore,
forever keeps me at a
distance without measure
far from the reach of your
shore.

#adrift

'She'

And yet she still walked into the storm, unafraid of the chaos, for it knew not of the struggle she had endured and won.

#she

LET IT BE

'Let It Be'

Let it go.
Upon every single breath
let the words you never speak
be the ones you scream instead.

Let it happen,
let the moment consume you whole,
so every painful memory that haunts you
can bring back the joy that sorrow stole.

Let me be the one,
the only one you see,
let me be the face that makes you smile
not the tears that make you leave.

#letitbe

'The Sea'

Amongst the wildest waters I move
unharmed, without fear I'll be
devoured complete. Such a force
am I beyond compare, each wave
begins and ends with me. Though
the tides are but a mass of
hands, they do not lead my path
astray, instead I wade into the
depths unknown, consuming all who
dare to block my way. For I am
vast just like the sea, master of
my own domain, should there come
a day that I am not, I'll accept
my fate and endure the pain.

#thesea

'So Very Deeply'

I meant nothing to
you, yet I still
can't help but feel
everything we were,
so very deeply,
it's as though you
never left me at
all.

A
GIRL

'A Girl'

A girl lay in bed
next to the warmth of
her lover, bleeding
tears that she cannot
control, he awakes
albeit only for a
second, but in that
moment she remembers
her well-rehearsed
smile.

#agirl

'Blank Spaces'

I see you in everyone that I
meet and yet they are not you,
in the same way I am not
myself, whenever we are apart.
Each nameless face like an
unforgiving tide which I swim
against, with all that I am, in
the hope that it may consume me
whole. For I am incomplete, as
is every moment that passes
without you. And there are
moments, endless moments, a
series of blank spaces which I
endure alone that have no
purpose other than to remind me
how truly lost I am without
you.

#bspaces

'Appreciate The Journey'

If you find someone
that   moves   you,
worry not about the
distance, appreciate
the journey instead.

MY SKY   MY STAR

'My Sky, My Star'

You are as vast as the sky, like a glorious star just beyond my reach. And yet I dream, knowing I would defy the sun to spend a lifetime within your presence, for your light is all I seek even though we remain eternally apart.

#msms

'I Sit And Wait'

I sit and wait

whilst others run

my body still

my fingers numb,

the darkness that surrounds me so

I wear it well

beneath my clothes.

And as I breathe with every breath

my spirit strong

unknown to death,

I still die inside almost every day

bereft of hope

I quietly pray.

For what am I without your love?

my constant thoughts awash with time,

viewing the world as though a stranger might

with eyes closed shut

I struggle blind.

And every time I think of you
be it a memory long forgotten or a feeling new,
the urge to move becomes harder to resist
tempted by Freedom as though I owned it
instead of it being something I'll always miss.

But who am I to think such things?
a lonely heart denied its wings,
for upon the ground is where I always dwell
my sky no more the day I fell.
And with every second that passes by
the nights seem longer within my mind,
for I cannot sleep like others do
no dreams have I
awash with you.

So I sit and wait
whilst others run
my body still
my fingers numb.

#isitandwait

You are stronger than you
think. Dig deep, find your
inner strength.

'I Circle In Your Orbit'

I circle in your orbit,
regardless of its
gravitational pull,
knowing you will keep me
at a distance, unaware
that you are my world and
always will be. Yet I
still circle.

#icircle

ONE LAST TIME

'One Last Time'

Give me all that you are, one
last time. I promise to fall
apart alone, behind a well-
rehearsed smile. There'll be no
more tears, none that you will
see, I'll be gracious as though
unbroken, even as I watch you
leave. The world will never
know of my scars or how I feel,
I'll wear them across my heart,
beneath my skin and pray to god
they never heal.

#olt

'Live For The Moment'

Yesterday I was,
tomorrow I will be,
but today I'll take my time
and just enjoy being me.

#lftm

'You Are The Sky'

I exist within your reach,
offering all that I am in
the hope you'll notice I'm
yours. For you are the
sky, a place so vast like
that of my love for you.
So I wander beneath every
passing cloud, allowing
the pieces of myself that
have always been yours to
be carried by the wind
until I no longer remain
alone - without you.

#thesky

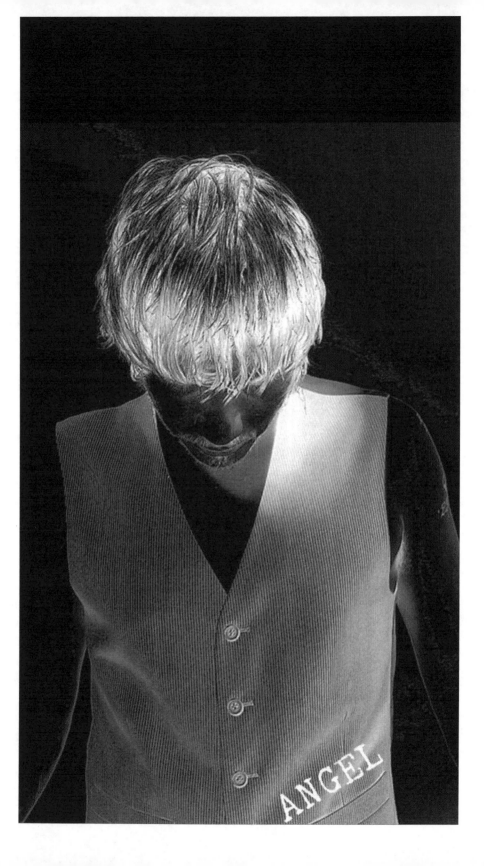

'Angel'

She always held onto him as
though their goodbye was
something she could continue
to live within, long after
the moment had passed. He
was her everything, in a
world where nothing else
mattered unless it happened
with him. The scars that
hung heavy upon her heart
seemed weightless whilst in
his arms, for she knew she
could give him her all and
he would keep it safe
forever.

#angel

'Wild'

Allow me the freedom to
roam your heart, so that
I may run wild through
every open door, in
search of you amongst
all the places you now
hide yourself from love.

#wild

FOREVER
GREEN

'Forever Green'

Forever green are my fields of hope
awash with trees and plants they grow,
I dwell within them without fear
unfazed by death
bereft of tears.

And with every breath I'm immune to sorrow
holding time within my hands
delaying all the unwanted tomorrows,
for as I Struggle within the raging storms
whilst they carry me along,
I still find control beyond the chaos
my only reassurance that I'm still strong,
allowing me to adjust the speed of my step
with every ebb and flow
until I'm dancing without knowing
no matter where I go.

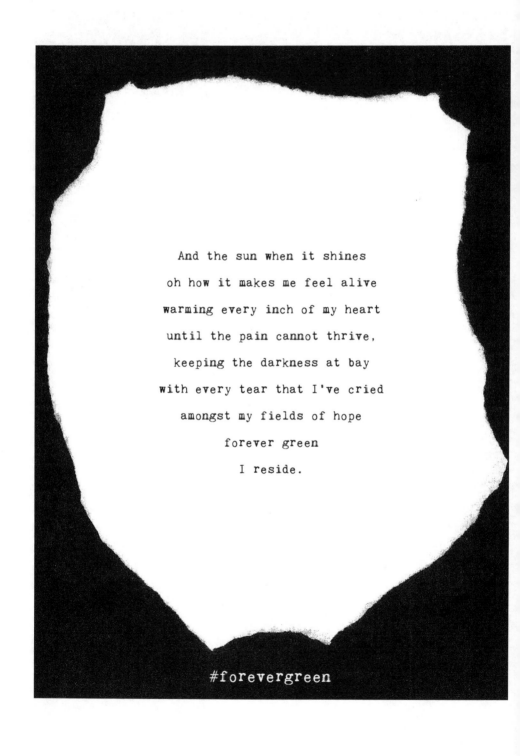

And the sun when it shines
oh how it makes me feel alive
warming every inch of my heart
until the pain cannot thrive,
keeping the darkness at bay
with every tear that I've cried
amongst my fields of hope
forever green
I reside.

#forevergreen

Smile often.

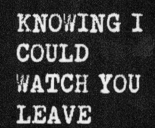

KNOWING I
COULD
WATCH YOU
LEAVE

'Knowing I Could
Watch You Leave'

Knowing I could
watch you leave,
lost forever to a
lifetime of goodbyes
is unfathomable,
like that of my love
for you.

#kicwyl

'A Reason To Change'

I am changeable and yet I
wouldn't change you, I would
change myself instead.
Aligning my heart with yours
until it felt like home. The
place where I belong,
knowing I could give you all
of me without asking for
anything in return. Except
you. Except us. Two souls
set adrift in an ocean so
vast, the tides forever in
our favour. Changing only to
bring us closer together in
the way I would change for
you.

#areasontochange

THIS
IS HOW
I MOVE

'This Is How I Move'

This is how I move
soft at first
then wild,
for I am all I'll ever need
yet I crave the things
that are not mine.
Such parting sorrow lives
amongst my broken smile,
though I'm as content as I am free
I still find myself dancing
in all the places
the shadows reach.

#howimove

YOU ARE
THE
OCEAN

'You Are The Ocean'

You are the ocean, each crashing wave that I swim toward regardless of the danger. For I would rather drown in love knowing that I gave it my all instead of treading water, forever lost at sea.

#theocean

ROAD
MAP

'Road Map'

You will always be my favourite part of the journey, regardless of its length. My eyes are open to the world and yet all I see is you as I walk the empty streets and endure the loneliness that they have to offer, knowing the scars I gain along the way are but a road map that leads me back home so I can remain forever within your heart.

#roadmap

'Smile'

Hear me not
and yet I speak,
be there no silence to halt my words
or enough tears to make me weep.
For my heart is still my own
regardless of the scars,
they are but wounds to remind me so
that the fight for love is hard.
And though I struggle every day
adorned in sorrow as though it were mine,
oh how I never falter whilst in its presence
for the fight is best fought
with that of a smile.

#smile

RECKLESS HEART

'Reckless Heart'

My heart is reckless when it comes
to you. It fears nothing. It takes
chances, unafraid of the dangers.
It defies the odds. For you are
worth the risk. Worth the fight.
And there will be a fight, most
days it will be an uphill struggle
because love is hard work, it's
never easy, not the kind that's
worth keeping. So I'll jump, I will
close my eyes and dive headfirst
into the abyss, knowing my reckless
heart will guide me to you as I
fall.

#reckless

NEXT
TO
YOU

'Next To You'

Next to you is where I lay

our bodies close and yet worlds apart,

I fear the silence for there are no words to say

that could ease the sorrow within my heart.

And yet I long to hold you near

to halt each tear before it forms,

what I would give to know that we still belong

and banish every broken thought.

Our fingertips that used to touch

are far beyond my current reach,

I now count the days that pass, for time is lost

to all the words we'll never speak.

Each memory I still own of you

is what I always treasure most,

your smile, your laugh, the way we were

is but a guiding light on my journeys path.

So next to you is where I'll lay

beside you without letting go,

no more am I until you awake

forever worlds apart

our bodies close.

#next2u

'Gathered'

Gathered, are all the
parts of me that now
remain. The jagged
edges. The broken pieces
that no longer fit into
the perfectly formed
corners of your heart,
in the way I once did.

#gathered

'The Fear'

In

your

final

hours,

may

the

pain

no

longer

hold

you

when

I

cannot.

#thefear

HIDDEN AWAY

'Hidden Away'

This is how it ends, without
a single breath exhaled, the
silence stealing all your
words, the ones you'll never
get to say. I see it in your
eyes amongst the tears you
hide away, convinced that
the world will see your
smile and believe that
everything's ok.

So you smile.

#hiddenaway

MONDAY	**FRAGILE**
TUESDAY	**FRAGILE**
WEDNESDAY	**FRAGILE**
THURSDAY	**FRAGILE**
FRIDAY	**FRAGILE**
SATURDAY	**FRAGILE**
SUNDAY	**FRAGILE**

PIECES

'Pieces'

Gather me within your arms
as though I belong, for I
am broken regardless of
how the pieces may fit.
Each fragment perfectly
aligned so you can't see
the cracks. But there are
scars, endless lines that
meet in the way we once
did, unprepared for the
moment when the splinters
become shards and it all
falls apart.

#pieces

'Grace'

What grace you have that I fall foul
stood before you yet my voice is lost,
be there a thousand words of love to quote
that tame the heart
and turn it soft.

Yet a single verse I can't recall
for your beauty leaves me at a loss,
oh how I pause within your presence so
unaware that for you no time has stopped.

And whilst I marvel at your smile
your lips like that of a perfect dream,
such a spell is cast upon my soul
that halts my voice so I cannot speak.

My every thought a nameless face
lost amongst a busy crowd,
oh what I would give for you to know my name
and say it once
to be heard aloud.

And it matters not to me at all
if I'm the only one to hear,
that you would speak of it would be enough
to warrant the distance
I still feel when you're near.

#grace

If you believe you can, you will.

DIAMONDS

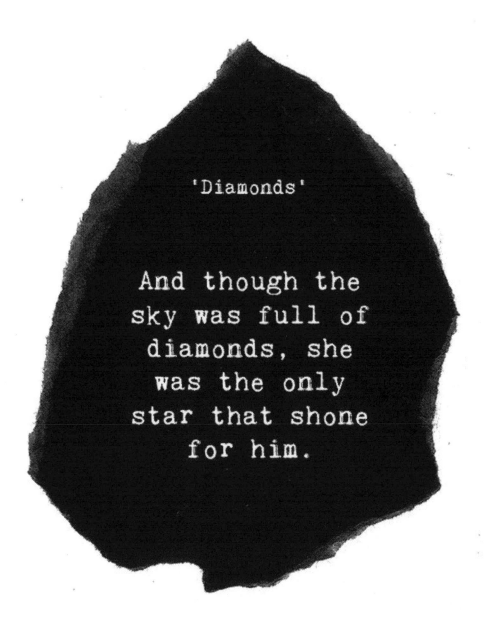

'Diamonds'

And though the
sky was full of
diamonds, she
was the only
star that shone
for him.

#diamonds

UNTIL THE END

'Until The End'

Like a plague upon my ears
I'm slowly deafened by the sound
the darkness hiding me within its light
I lay unnoticed upon the ground.

And as my body begins to ache
from the pain that taunts it so
I push far beyond the realms of sleep
rejecting its warm and loving glow.

For life would lose all hope and meaning
If I gave it up so fast
I'd rather breathe my final breath
knowing I fought to earn my battle scars.

So when death slowly descends
like a Phoenix from the skies
I shall make it wait an eternity whilst in my presence
and never dare to close my eyes.

#theend

BURNT

'Burnt'

My life is now a series
of circles in which I
move alone. The journey
endless like that of the
love I hold within my
heart, only for you, in
the hope we will once
again collide in the most
beautifulest of ways.

So I circle.

#burnt

FOUND MYSELF
FOUND YOU

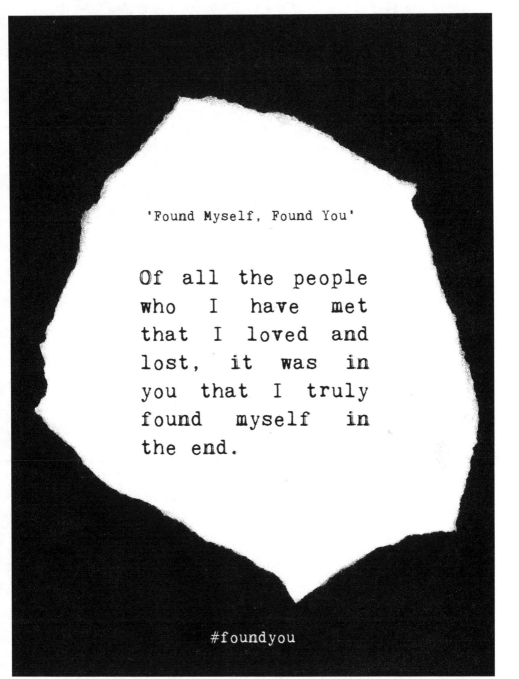

'Found Myself, Found You'

Of all the people
who I have met
that I loved and
lost, it was in
you that I truly
found myself in
the end.

#foundyou

'Wide Awake'

Place your hand within mine
so the world can see that I
am yours. For it matters not
to me at all what lies ahead
if I'm with you. Our fingers
interlocked shall become the
bond this world can never
break. Each day may end but
I'll never sleep, instead I
will live each dream with
you whilst I'm wide awake.

#wideawake

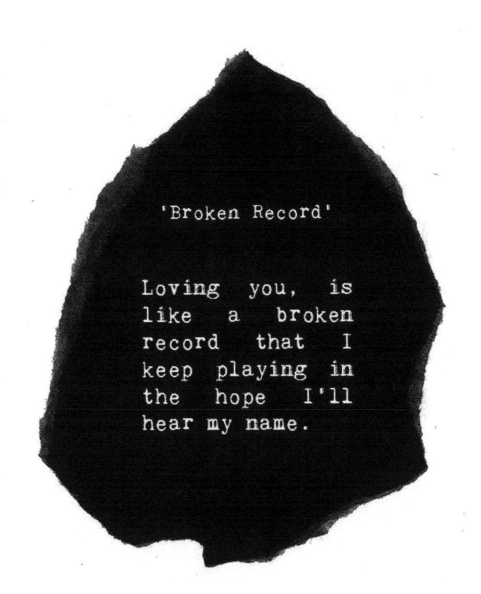

'Broken Record'

Loving you, is like a broken record that I keep playing in the hope I'll hear my name.

#brokenrecord

THESE ARE
NOT MY
WORDS

'These Are Not My Words'

These are not my words, they belong to someone else, written with another heart in mind yet I could only see myself. From their beautiful opening lines to the last uplifting verse, it's as though heaven sang a song of love and it was only my name I heard. For I've imagined every day, what it would be like to hear the words as they were said, how I'd revel in their glory instead of dwelling on regret, then I wouldn't feel so lonely with empty thoughts left in my head, wanting to be the person that people notice and not the one they now forget.

#tanmw

'Fires'

Now's not the time
nor shall it ever be,
to fight the fires that burn
with the fires that be.
Though there lives a courage in the heart
of every woman and man
to honour and defend their holy land,
let us pause for a moment
and in that moment just be,
without the need to harm another
because of their colour or creed
or a faith they belong to
that offers them the hope that they need
a shelter from the fires that burn
lit by the fires that be.

#fires

I SHALL WALK THIS PATH

'I Shall Walk This Path'

I shall walk this path
with my head held high,
leaving the pain far behind me
amongst all the tears that I've cried.
For the sorrow from my past
that always brings me to my knees,
is but a memory long forgotten
upon every breath that I breathe.
And the journey ahead
although I walk it alone,
shall become a distance forever travelled
until I find my way home.
Every step a new beginning
erasing all the scars from my heart,
turning all the wrongs into rights
I shall walk this path.

#ishallwalk

'Such Precious Things'

"Because I often find myself
comparing people to flowers."

Such precious things lead fragile lives
and yet they live out in plain sight,
I see them fade before my very eyes
in the way an unwanted flower might.
Each dainty leaf, once tended to
now sits left to wither
like forgotten things do,
be it a beautiful rose
in the fullest of bloom
or a wild flower gone wild
awaiting its groom.
How they dwell all alone
devoid of attention,
no longer seen as they disappear
without the slightest mention.
And in their place sits another
such a beauty to behold,
unaware of how much it will be treasured
for it shall never be told.

#precious

'Stones'

I carry the weight of my worries

as though they were stones,

each one a memory collected

that weighs me down.

Although my pockets remain full

set to overflow,

I always find myself gathering stones

wherever I roam.

#stones

'Bloom'

And yet the sun
still shines as
the spring flowers
bloom, unaware
that beauty has no
purpose once love
is removed.

#bloom

PETRICHOR

'Petrichor'

As vast as the world may seem,
you will always be my final
destination. Though I wander, I
often find myself stood beneath
your sky undeterred by the rain,
however it may fall. The sweet
scent of your presence lingering
in the air long after you have
gone, a reminder that you are
mine and I am yours regardless of
the distance that divides us.

#petrichor

'The Fall'

Oh how I often linger at the edge without regret, unaware of the fall beneath my feet. For nothing have I but time alone, to count the days until we finally meet. No wings have I that allow me flight, only tears and memories to weigh me down, one day I'll find the courage within myself, walking far beyond the edge, knowing I will be returning back home - to you.

#thefall

A
DARKENED
CLOUD

'A Darkened Cloud'

Fortune favours those that love
or so it seems until all is lost,
every sun filled dream
where once shone hope
can become a darkened cloud
that lingers close.

Its presence such a heavy weight
all The broken hearts lay buried deep
forced to grieve awash with endless thoughts
of constant rain without reprieve.

And the visions which they must endure
that wound and maim with every breath
offer no promise to those that seek them out
but endless days of emptiness.

Each painful cut
a lasting scar
forcing the journey, no longer travelled
forever adrift from its path,
and yet the darkened cloud remains tethered
by all the ties that bind
its victim helplessly watching as it hovers to another
gaining a distance, that can never be recovered
regardless of time.

#adarkenedcloud

'Stars'

To the stars I travel a weary soul
my wings unravelled for the journey home,
just beyond the skyline
where all the angels gather,
I'll be the sunrise come the morning
to remind the whole world that I mattered.

#stars

'Slow Dance'

Oh how you make my
heart race, as
though I'm slow
dancing with you
in my arms to a
song that never
ends.

#slowdance

BATTLE SCARS

'Battle Scars'

Such a sea of bodies weigh me down
their tide so strong I'm dragged beneath,
be there no silence here but that of sound
its constant voice is all I hear.
And yet I wade into the deep
the devil's wrath within my veins,
oh how I push against the fires that burn
regardless of their violent flames.
For what am I if nothing more
than all the things I've come to fear,
I'd rather dance a thousand times with death
then be denied each moment
only to watch it disappear.
So I wage my wars with caution not
seeking darkness out at unknown depths,
knowing every scar I earn cannot erase
the pain I felt the day you left.
And though a shield is placed around my heart
it offers nothing more than that of time,
for I am lost to every empty thought
that now lives forever within my mind.

#battlescars

'My Angel'

I no longer see beauty
regardless of the times I've
searched for it in the hope I
would find you. For you are not
mine nor will you ever be.
Instead you belong to the
clouds. Unobtainable. Eternally
beyond my reach. And though I
spend my days lost within a
lifetime of perfectly formed
memories, they will never be
enough because they are not you.
They are not us. So I wander.
Drawn to all the places that
were once filled with you, only
to find they now remain
permanently empty.

#myangel

'If The World Should Cease To Be'

If the world should cease to be
even though my eyes aren't closed,
let time pause so I can live within it forever
knowing I shall never be alone.

For all the memories that are mine
may they carry me along,
recalling you back from beyond my reach
to where you once belonged.

Then I'd never have to worry
as each day begins anew,
spared the pain of every empty tomorrow
that ends the second it begins without you.

For you are the sunshine I always seek

beyond the clouds up in the sky,

forced to live my life owning nothing but sorrow

that sits like a fog before my eyes.

Spending every second in a world ruled by darkness

regardless of the light,

oh how I often dream of heaven

now that you're one of god's angels,

as I lay alone in bed every night.

And though I carry on believing

that you're right here by my side,

I will forever be an empty hearted vessel

adrift at sea

bereft of tide.

#itwsctb

Positivity should always
be the order of the day.

Gentle

'Gentle'

Gentle, like the birds
that fly is how you
calm my ferocious mind.
I feel such warmth
every time we share a
long embrace, knowing I
can close my eyes and
pretend you're mine.

#gentle

'Infinity'

Amidst the wreck and ruin lay
two hearts that loved without regret,
though their fingertips never touched at all,
may they find each other
in the loving arms of death.

#infinity

'Softly Into The Night'

Softly into the night we
go, every footstep
stolen without trace.
Empty are the days that
lay ahead, and yet they
carry such a heavy
weight. In shades of
black and grey they
pass, each one longer
than the last, until
time exists only to
remind us so, how much
it hurts to endure the
loss of our loved ones
alone. As softly into
the night they go.

#sitn

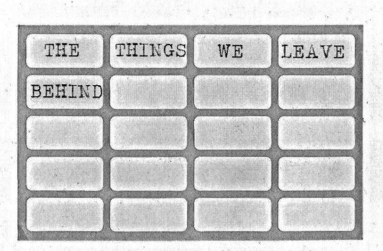

'The Things We Leave Behind'

She would always leave pieces of
herself in the places that
mattered the most, regardless of
how heavy the distance sat upon
her inconsolable heart. Knowing
she belonged to something, even
if belonging meant feeling lost
wherever life would lead her,
was how she had learned to
breathe. And although it left
her broken, each piece painfully
sharp, she found comfort amongst
the memories for they reminded
her of home, and it was as
though she had never truly left
at all.

#ttwlb

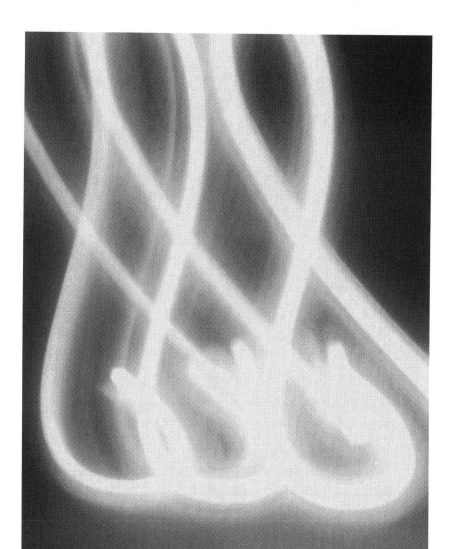

I AM
KING

'I Am King'

Such a force exists inside of me
a strength of which I can't contain,
be there monsters upon my every path
yet I walk undeterred
without pause or refrain.
For I am king of all I own
master of my own domain,
should a darkness come to rule my heart
it shall know of me
and fear my name.

#iamking

THE CROW

'The Crow'

Oh how the crow does
dance above me so, as it
moves in rhythm with the
calming winds. Be its
feathered wings that of
loving hands, that wave
farewell as I watch it
leave.

#thecrow

I FOUND
MYSELF
TODAY

'I Found Myself Today'

I found myself today

as though I'd always been lost,

stood in a room adorned with angels

bathed in gods forgiving gloss.

And as silent as it seemed

I still heard their voices within my mind,

opening my eyes to a world filled with promise

instead of always being forced to look upon it blind.

And as I gazed upon them so

behind a veil of foggy haze,

I felt the fires that used to burn

slowly ebb away and fade.

For as the moment grew and grew

so the pain eased within my chest,

such a chorus of sound erupted before me

and stole my every waking breath.

And as I fell down to my knees
awash with glory like it had always been mine,
I saw my life albeit moving in slow motion
flash before my very eyes.
Every vision like a sea of forever
flowing through the boroughs of my mind,
oh how I gained a comfort once thought stolen
by the loneliness of time.
And as the tears streamed down my face
so the memories flooded back,
I surrendered to the moment embracing it completely
its vibrant colours my every shade of black.
Be it a glorious green
or a heavenly blue,
I saw such hope as though I'd always owned it
and marvelled at the view.
For I knew deep down inside
feeling the darkness fade away,
although I once was lost
I found myself today.

#ifoundmyself

Always be yourself, not
what other people want you
to be.

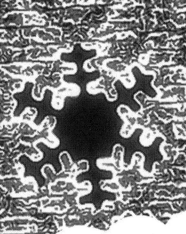

MORNING
SUN

'Morning Sun'

Oh morning sun

how you always greet me so,

allowing me to bask within your loving

you fill my heart until it glows.

And I sometimes often wonder

whilst I sit beneath your sky,

do you ever realise how much I adore you

with every cloud that passes by?

And I can feel your warmth upon me

even when my eyes are closed,

it's like the world and all its worries

seem to stop like they have froze,

removing all the emptiness that dwells within me

until I never feel alone.

And I know that once the day ends

the moon will come and take your place,

but I'll be peacefully sleeping away the hours

awash with fond memories of your face.

#morningsun

I
DARE
NOT
DREAM

'I Dare Not Dream'

Though my eyes are closed, I dare not dream. For if I awake to find you are not mine, what use are dreams to me?

'Jagged Edges'

Across jagged edges
I run my fingers free,
unaware of all the pain
or how they slowly bleed.
Lost amongst everlasting thoughts
of how you swore you'd never leave,
I find myself drawn to jagged edges
my fingers running free.

#jaggededges

'God'

To God, to God I'll
finally go, he'll ease
the pain and cleanse my
soul. My father, my
brother, my faithful
friend, I will truly
know his name come
journeys end.

#god

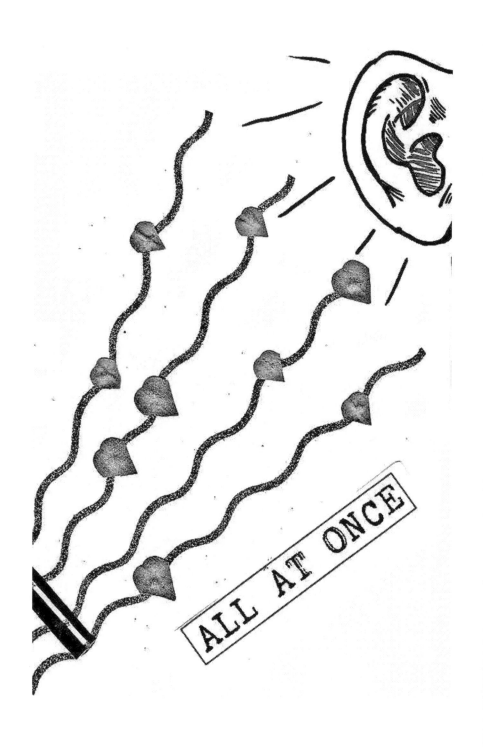

'All At Once'

Oh distant voices upon my ears
I hear your words in perfect tones
come infect my heart with your sense of joy
for life has left me all alone.

And the silence that often owns my thoughts
the ones I've tried to keep at bay
oh how your sounds overwhelm them all at once
slowly delaying the pain until they cannot stay.

But as I submit myself to your choral song
still the chains of life seem to bind me so
pulling tighter and tighter until I can barely breathe
their grip everlasting so as to never let go.

Oh what of me that I am torn
the weight of the world upon my body so
I hear your song and inside I'm as free as a bird
flying high without fear
far from the worries below.

And with every day that passes by
I still listen with a strength renewed
reaching out in hope towards a sombre sky
awash with tears I cannot move.

Oh voices how I pray to thee
may you come all at once and never leave
for time is all I'll ever own
be it bearable within your presence
I wouldn't want to live within it alone.

#allatonce

You hear more
when you truly listen.

NADINE SAOUD

27/11/89 - 1/5/13

'Today Was But A Dream'

- Dedicated to Nadine Saoud -

Today my whole world was that of a dream
and yet as it began like any other
somehow it didn't seem real,
for I could feel in my heart
as it awoke from its sleep
there lived within me an unmentionable sorrow
that just wouldn't leave.

And though the skyline was perfect
awash with every kind of blue,
It still lacked the warmth I'd come to treasure
as the sun came into view.
Staring at the clouds high above me
as they moved in their glorious domain
I couldn't help but gaze at them as if forever
their beauty my only distraction from the pain.

And as I walked from street to street
my thoughts as lost as they could be
my body being pulled along by a tide of strangers
In a never ending sea,
I found myself thinking of the ones that I loved the most
all those present and departed
faraway and close.

And then in an instant I knew
without the words being said
hearing the familiar sound of your voice
like a distant thought inside my head.
As you spoke in a calm and comforting way
to reassure me you were fine, and it would all be ok
I couldn't help but cry
unable to deal with it all
for the world I thought once big
seemed as dark as it did small.

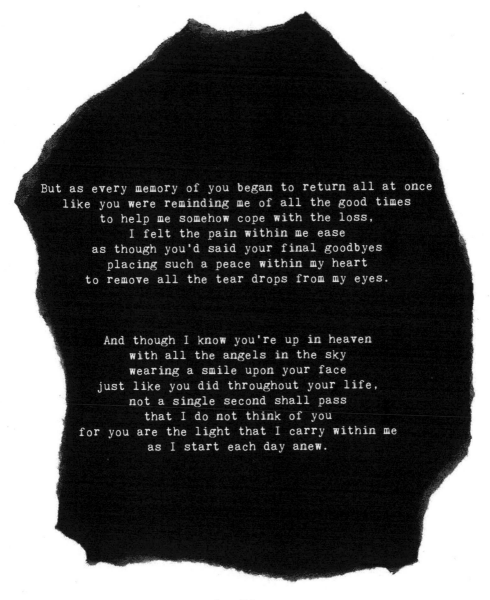

But as every memory of you began to return all at once
like you were reminding me of all the good times
to help me somehow cope with the loss,
I felt the pain within me ease
as though you'd said your final goodbyes
placing such a peace within my heart
to remove all the tear drops from my eyes.

And though I know you're up in heaven
with all the angels in the sky
wearing a smile upon your face
just like you did throughout your life,
not a single second shall pass
that I do not think of you
for you are the light that I carry within me
as I start each day anew.

#nadine

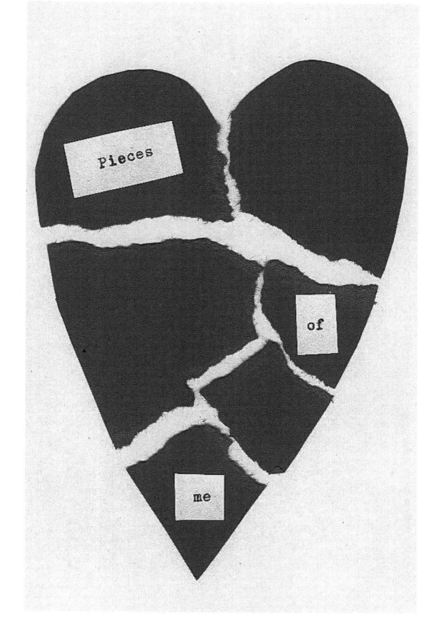

'Pieces Of Me'

I still leave the
pieces of my broken
heart in all the
places that we once
belonged, in the hope
you'll return one day
and see I never truly
left.

#piecesofme

NIGHT

AND DAY

'Night And Day'

If I am but a night sky, may you
always be the early morning sunrise
that I seek. A reminder of what was,
so I am not completely alone in this
world. Knowing that I could lose
myself whilst in your presence
regardless of consequence, just to
have you look at me in the way I look
at you, is all that I crave. Our two
halves forming a perfect circle,
together as one yet always apart. And
though my body tires, I know not of
sleep, for what use are dreams if when
you awake your eyes still remain
closed, so that all you ever see is
darkness.

#nandd

'Masquerade'

Place your hands
around my heart, for
I own scars that will
not heal. Interlock
your fingers tight,
I'll wear a smile to
hide the tears.

#masquerade

STRANGERS

'Strangers'

I am but a stranger to you
every time that we meet,
feeling that familiar sideways glance
as you pass me on the street.
No Hello
or goodbye
my life a loop of constant repeats,
forever moving forwards
without pausing
to acknowledge and greet.
Yet I like to think as we pass
time slows down as if stopped,
and in that second
we are no longer strangers
but dreamers, who dream of defying the odds.

#strangers

BROKEN

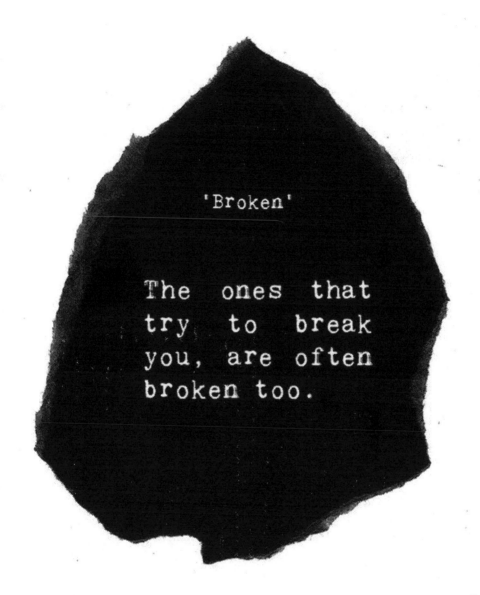

'Broken'

The ones that
try to break
you, are often
broken too.

#broken

AN OLD FLAME

'An Old Flame'

I see sorrow everywhere I
go. It often greets me like
an old flame as though we
were once lovers, torn apart
only to be reunited in the
most tragic of ways. And
though I fear it's darkness,
that welcoming smile, I will
always be drawn to it
regardless of the times I
end up getting burnt, it's
fire my sanctuary from a
world I cannot escape.

#anoldflame

'I Am But A Leaf'

I am but a leaf, without
the shelter of its tree,
dragged forever by the
wind, as violent as it
may be. And though I
move within the breeze,
so graceful and free,
beauty hides the tears I
cry, that force me to my
knees, until I am
nothing but a leaf,
without the shelter of
its tree.

#iamaleaf

WITHIN MY HANDS

'Within My Hands'

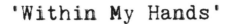

Within my hands I hold the light
Its rays of hope
shine strong and bright,
the darkness of which I dare not speak
still taunts me although it cannot reach.
And every time I think of you
my thoughts awash with memories gone
the light within my hands grows weak
to remind me of where I once belonged.

#myhands

BEAUTIFUL

'Beautiful'

One day it will stop. The ache in your heart will cease and you will finally be free from the pain. It won't be easy though. There will be moments where you will feel like you are alone and the world is against you, a rising tide moving faster than you could possibly swim. Worry not my dear, for you are beautiful and beautiful things never die, instead they bloom into something better. So use that tide, let it push you, allow it to take you where you need to be. And when you arrive, smile to let the world know that even though it was a struggle, you still fought the fight and won.

#beautiful

NEVER BE AFRAID

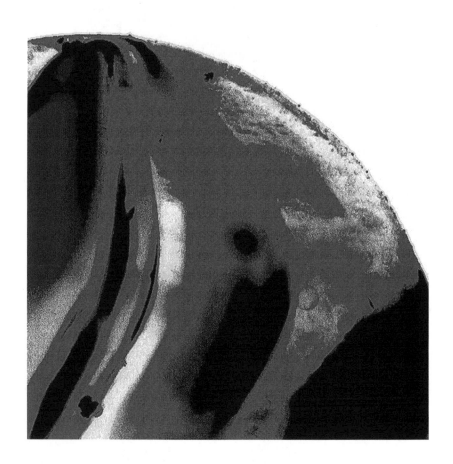

'Never Be Afraid'

Never be afraid, when
it comes to love. It
just takes the right
kind of person, to say
the right kind of
words that open your
eyes to a world in
which you've always
belonged.

I STILL AWAKE EACH NIGHT

'I Still Awake Each Night'

I still awake each night
awash with broken hearted dreams,
wanting love to feel my never ending sorrow
as it saves me from these tears.
For this darkness that I own
the kind that taunts me whilst I grieve,
was born the day I embraced forever
and was forced to watch it leave.
And I know that come the morning
when the sun lights up the sky,
the world will smile at me regardless
of all the tears it's made me cry.

#isaen

SILHOUETTE

'Silhouette'

When she is in my presence,
I'm attracted to the light
that floods from her
silhouette as though she were
a midnight sky and my heart
knew only how to worship the
stars.

#silhouette

'Let It Rain'

Let there be rain
let it fall all at once,
be there no rivers that can contain it
or a tide to slow its force.
May it flow through every valley
towards the promise of the sea,
soft and gentle
yet at times ferocious,
like the way you make me feel.
For I am loved whilst in your waters
set adrift
only to be pulled back to shore,
knowing that regardless of our distance
still the currents draw us near.
And though there will be days of constant sunshine
not a cloud up in the sky,
I'll always look in hope that when I find one
it shall rain
and once again
you'll be mine.

#letitrain

'Wings'

I won't fall for
you from heights
I'm too afraid to
climb, unless you
place your wings
around my heart, so
when I jump, I do
so knowing that you
are truly mine.

#wings

'I Have Dreamt'

I have dreamt of many things
all the stars and how they shine,
the promise of a perfect sunrise
like god is stood before my eyes.
I have lived a thousand lives
yet none of them were mine,
they belonged to another
in the way that you do
regardless of the times I've died inside.

#ihavedreamt

'Roots'

You shall always be the
garden in which I sow my
seeds of hope, knowing
their roots will forever
remain nourished and
grow into beautiful
flowers regardless of
the weather they endure.

#roots

FOOTPRINTS
IN THE SAND

'Footprints In The Sand'

I often wander through
the forgotten parts of
my mind in the hope I'll
find you. Our unfinished
journey comparable to
that of footprints in
the sand, held at the
mercy of the sea, each
crashing wave as
forgiving as my love is
for you.

So I wander.

#footprints

THE
DANCE

'The Dance'

This is how I move, as
though in a well-rehearsed
dance, knowing you will
always be the rhythm to
which I align my
uncontrollable heart.

#thedance

THE STRUGGLE

'The Struggle'

If the resilience of a broken heart can
be compared to anything, offering hope
to the recently wounded, let it be to
that of the struggle that follows. There
will be a struggle, as much as you try
and hide it, you will ache in places you
never thought possible and feel it all
so very deeply. But it is from the pain
that you will find your inner strength.
Just because you are broken doesn't mean
you can't be fixed. Yes, there will be
scars, each one a reminder of how much
love hurt you, but it did you a favour,
it taught you a valuable lesson, made
you stronger. The next time you give
your heart to someone completely it will
be because they've seen your scars and
still love you regardless, and from that
you will know that it was all
worthwhile, the path … the journey … the
struggle.

#thestruggle

ABOUT THE AUTHOR

James grew up in an area in Northampton aptly named 'Poets Corner', unbeknownst that poetry was to become a huge part of his life. Having no prior interest in the subject matter in his younger years, James discovered the wonders of writing in his twenties. Mixing his own thoughts and emotions with classical and instrumental film scores, he realised for the first time in his life that there was more to writing than met the eye. With no real influences or coming from a writing background, James' enthusiasm grew and grew and it was full steam ahead — with no turning back!

Not content with writing words for his own amusement, he continued to test the boundaries — to great effect. Using his new found love for writing and his in depth knowledge of social networking sites, his resourcefulness resulted in success.

Attracting a lot of attention over the years, James and his works have covered a wide range of different media platforms. With his works, he has been featured in various UK and International magazines and newspapers and has been featured on various radio stations in the UK and the Netherlands including the BBC (where he is a part of the newspaper review team). His words have been adapted and performed by many musicians and vocalists, with many of them gaining a lot of airplay on multiple radio stations.

With various US/UK Actors and Actresses voicing his poetry, James is taking his words to a whole new level.

His debut book 'In between the Lines' is currently available to buy on Amazon and Kindle, and is also available to read for free in various schools, colleges, universities and libraries in the UK, Ireland and America.

For News, YouTube covers, Photography, Poetry and Magazine and Radio appearances you can keep up to date with James and his works by using any of the following sites:

Official website:

http://jamesmcinerney.wix.com/poetry

YouTube:

http://www.youtube.com/user/millsmc1977

Facebook:

https://www.facebook.com/groups/JamesTMcInerney/

Twitter:
@millsmc07

Instagram:
@millsmc07

Tumblr:
borntobeapoet2015

Snapchat:
Jeeter77

Email:
jeeter77@gmail.com

Made in the USA
Charleston, SC
11 August 2016